World of Islam

The Muslim World: An Overview

MASON CREST PUBLISHERS
PHILADELPHIA

World of Islam

World of Islam

The Muslim World: An Overview

DOROTHY KAVANAUGH

Editorial Consultants: Foreign Policy Research Institute, Philadelphia, PA

Mason Crest Publishers
370 Reed Road
Broomall, PA 19008
www.masoncrest.com

First printing

1 3 5 7 9 8 6 4 2

Library of Congress Cataloging-in-Publication Data

Kavanaugh, Dorothy, 1969-
  The Muslim world : an overview / Dorothy Kavanaugh.
      p. cm. — (World of Islam)
  ISBN 978-1-4222-0532-7 (hardcover)
  ISBN 978-1-4222-0805-2 (pbk.)
  1. Islam—20th century—Juvenile literature. 2. Islam—History—Juvenile literature.
  3. Muslims—History—Juvenile literature. 4. Islam—Customs and practices—Juvenile literature.
  5. Muslims—Social life and customs—Juvenile literature. I. Title.
  BP163.K387 2008
  297.09—dc22
                          2008042170

Dorothy Kavanaugh is a freelance writer whose books include *Islam, Christianity, and Judaism* (2004), *Islam in Africa* (2006), and *Islamic Festivals and Celebrations* (2010). She lives near Philadelphia.

Table of Contents

What Is Islam?

*I*slam is one of the world's three major monotheistic faiths, along with Judaism and Christianity. Across the globe, there are about 1.3 billion Muslims, as followers of Islam are called. Muslims come from a variety of ethnic backgrounds and live in diverse societies. Furthermore, Islam is not monolithic, but has distinct branches and sects with somewhat differing traditions, ritual practices, and doctrines. Nonetheless, Muslims consider themselves united as part of a worldwide community of believers called the umma. All committed Muslims share certain core beliefs.

Origins of Islam

The birth of Islam can be traced to the seventh century C.E., on the Arabian Peninsula in what is now Saudi Arabia. Around the year 610, Muslims believe, an angel began to deliver messages

An ornate mosque, or Muslim house of worship, in Putrajaya, Malaysia. About 25 percent of the world's population—some 1.3 billion people—identify themselves as Muslims, or followers of Islam. Muslim communities can be found in practically every country around the world.

from God to a wealthy Arab merchant named Muhammad ibn Abd Allah. According to Muslim belief, the angel explained that there is only one God, Allah, and that all people should submit to Allah's will. (The word *Islam* is derived from the Arabic verb *aslama*, which means "to submit.") The angel told Muhammad how people should worship Allah, and how they should live their lives, Muslims believe. The angel then instructed Muhammad to proclaim this message to others.

At the time Muhammad lived in Mecca, an important city in the western part of the Arabian Peninsula. Meccans—as well as other Arabs of this period—were polytheistic. Mecca was the site of an important shrine, the Kaaba, which contained numerous idols. Pilgrims flocked to the city to worship these idols, and Mecca's merchants grew wealthy catering to the pilgrims' needs. For commercial as well as religious reasons, therefore, many Meccans would not be receptive to Muhammad's teachings.

For several years, apparently, Muhammad shared the messages he claimed to receive from Allah only with family members and close friends. Around 613, however, he began to speak publicly about Allah. He told the people to stop worshipping idols and to worship only Allah. He condemned unjust practices in Meccan society. He said that the wealthy should share their money with the poor.

Gradually, over the course of years, Muhammad attracted a small but significant circle of followers. Most Meccans rejected his teachings, however. Muhammad and his followers were harassed, ostracized, and threatened with violence.

Finally, in 622, Muhammad and a group of approximately 200 followers fled Mecca for the city of Yathrib, which was later renamed Medina. This journey, known as the *hijra*, was an important milestone in the history of Islam and marks the beginning of the Islamic calendar. Muhammad was able to preach

This 19th century painting by the French artist Alphonse Etienne Dinet shows Medina, the city where Muhammad established the first Muslim community in 622 C.E.

freely in Medina. Many people there accepted Muhammad's teachings, and he soon became the community's spiritual and political leader.

For several years, Mecca and Medina fought a war. Muhammad's followers eventually gained the upper hand, and in January of 630 Muhammad led a large army to Mecca. The city's dispirited residents surrendered without a fight. Afterward, many Meccans converted to Islam, as did the members of other Arab tribes who lived around the city.

By 632, when Muhammad died, Muslims controlled the territory around Mecca and Medina, as well as much of the Arabian Peninsula. In the decades that followed, Islam would spread rapidly through conquest as well as voluntary conversion.

The Qur'an, Islam's Holy Scripture

Islam's sacred scripture, the Qur'an, is the most important source of spiritual doctrine for Muslims. Muslims believe the Qur'an contains the exact messages that Muhammad received from Allah in the Arabic language. The Qur'an is therefore not simply the word of God, but God's very words.

Yet the words of the Qur'an were not written down during the lifetime of Muhammad, who could neither read nor write. Rather, Muhammad recited the messages and told his followers to memorize them. Over the years, some messages were written down on pieces of bone or scraps of paper. Others were passed down orally. As a result, there were many variant texts, though these have been suppressed and Muslims deny they ever existed.

The task of compiling an authoritative Qur'an—based on a review of the texts by Muhammad's closest surviving followers (known as the Companions) and other Muslim leaders—was only begun a dozen years after Muhammad's death. This is one reason Western scholars doubt the assertion by mainstream Muslims that the Qur'an is exactly as recited during Muhammad's lifetime.

The Qur'an includes the messages that Muslims believe Allah gave to Muhammad between 610 and 632 C.E. An authoritative written version of the text was not created until around 654, during the reign of the third caliph, Uthman ibn Affan.

(The Qur'an also contains certain internal inconsistencies, and late-seventh-century and eighth-century copies with slight variations have been discovered.) Today, however, all Muslims use the same Qur'an.

The Qur'an contains 114 chapters, called *suras*. After the first chapter, the *suras* are organized roughly according to length, from longest to shortest. The first chapter is called al-Fatiha ("The Opening"), and it is a short chapter that Muslims recite during each of their five daily prayers. Every *sura* is divided into verses called *ayat*. Chapters in the Qur'an address a variety of issues, including Allah and creation, Muhammad as a spiritual and political leader, the teachings of other prophets (these include important figures from the Judeo-Christian tradition, such as Abraham, Moses, and Jesus), and Allah's requirements for society in general.

Although the Qur'an forms the basis of Islamic doctrine, it does not contain much information about specific religious practices. For example, the Qur'an tells Muslims that they must pray, but it does not explain exactly how a Muslim should pray. Many of the specific religious practices associated with Islam are derived from the Hadith. This is a collection of the sayings and actions of Muhammad and the Companions.

The Hadith and the Sunna

Muhammad's followers recorded his statements, religious instructions, and actions. Collectively, these are known as the Hadith. (Each individual story is also called a Hadith.) The Hadith are second only to the Qur'an as a source of Islamic doctrine. These anecdotes are used to show Muslims how Muhammad interpreted Allah's teachings in his own life.

Unlike the Qur'an, there is no absolute canon of Hadith. Many stories were preserved, but some are considered inaccurate.

Others are accepted by certain Muslim sects but not by others. By the ninth century, approximately 250 years after Muhammad's death, Muslim scholars had compiled four sets of Hadith considered legitimate. These were collected, checked, validated, and compiled by Muhammad Ibn Ismail al-Bukhari (809–870); Muslim Ibn al-Hajjaj (817–876); Sulaiman Ibn Ash'ath, also known as Abu Dawud (817–888); and Muhammad Ibn Zayid (824–915).

Two collections of Hadith are considered the most authoritative. Al-Bukhari, the most famous collector of Hadith, reviewed approximately a half-million sayings but found only about 7,500 to be valid. And each saying that Muslim Ibn al-Hajjaj validated is said to be directly traceable to someone who either heard what Muhammad said or who witnessed what Muhammad did.

The Hadith are important because they provide specific religious and social guidance that Muslims may apply to their daily lives. The example of Muhammad, as revealed through the Hadith, is known as the *Sunna* (Arabic for "path"). For example, the Qur'an tells Muslims that they have certain obligations: to be charitable to others, to perform daily prayers, to pay a tax for the benefit of the Muslim state, and to make decisions as a community. The ways in which these things should be done are found in the Sunna.

The Five Pillars of Islam

Islam's five fundamental obligations include the profession of faith (*shahada*), daily prayer (*salat*), charitable giving (*zakat*), fasting during the month of Ramadan (*sawm*), and the pilgrimage to Mecca (*hajj*).

The profession of faith—"There is no god but Allah, and Muhammad is His messenger"—is required of anyone who

A Muslim man performs morning prayers in Srinagar, India. Daily prayer is one of the five pillars, or essential requirements, of Islam.

Chinese Muslims leave the Id Kah Mosque in Kashgar, Xinjiang province, after a Ramadan service. Fasting during Ramadan is meant to challenge Muslims to consider their own lives and think about whether they are fully submitting to Allah's will on a daily basis.

wishes to join the Muslim community. Muslims profess their faith during their daily prayers.

All Muslims are supposed to pray five times daily, at dawn, noon, mid-afternoon, sunset, and night. Before performing these prayers, Muslims must clean and purify themselves. When Muslims pray, they turn toward the Kaaba, in Mecca. According to Muslim tradition, the Kaaba was originally built by Adam as a shrine to God; after it was destroyed in the Great Flood, it was rebuilt by Abraham and his son Ishmael, from whom Arabs trace their ancestry. Pagan Arab tribes were said to have defiled the shrine by filling it with idols, until the prophet Muhammad captured Mecca, destroyed the idols, and rededicated the Kaaba to God. To Muslims, the Kaaba is the holiest place on earth. This shrine symbolizes the unity of the worldwide Muslim community, the *umma*.

For the most part, Muslims perform their daily prayers alone or in small groups. However, an entire Muslim community is expected to meet at noon on Fridays in their mosque, or place of worship. A religious leader, called an imam, leads the congregational prayer. At the mosque, worshippers arrange themselves in rows so that they may kneel and bow without touching anyone around them. In some Muslim communities, women pray separately from men.

The third pillar of Islam is the obligation of Muslims to give to charity. The requirement that Muslims must share with the poor is stressed throughout the Qur'an. There are two forms of charitable giving: a mandatory tax (*zakat*) and voluntary almsgiving (*sadaqa*). However, the Qur'an does not contain specific guidelines for how much one should give or how this obligation should be enforced. The amount and manner of giving has been the subject of much debate and study over the centuries. Today, the amount of the tax varies, depending on where a Muslim lives.

The fourth pillar of Islam is the fast during the month of Ramadan. Ramadan is one of the 12 months of the Islamic lunar calendar. Because the lunar calendar follows the phases of the moon rather than the earth's revolution around the sun, the length of a lunar year is 354 or 355 days, 10 or 11 days shorter than the solar 365-day calendar. Therefore, Ramadan begins on different dates each year. Ramadan is considered a sacred month because Muslims believe it was during this month that Muhammad received his first revelations from Allah.

During Ramadan, Muslims must refrain from eating and other pleasures from daybreak to sundown each day. The fast is supposed to help Muslims build physical and spiritual discipline, to serve as a reminder of the trials of the poor, and to build a sense of unity among all Muslims. At the end of Ramadan, worshippers celebrate with a three-day holiday known as Eid al-Fitr.

The fifth pillar of Islam requires all Muslims to make a pilgrimage to Mecca at least once in their lives, if they are physically and financially able to do so. The hajj is considered one of the most unifying experiences of the Islamic faith. Muslims from all walks of life make the journey to Mecca, and all are considered equal when they are on the hajj. During the hajj Muslim pilgrims perform a variety of rituals and ceremonies. These are intended to help them set aside their worldly concerns and draw closer to Allah.

The Rise of Islamism

The belief that religion cannot be separated from any other part of life was an important part of the teachings of the prophet Muhammad in the seventh century, and for hundreds of years this belief buttressed a powerful Islamic civilization that extended its power through the Middle East and into Asia, Africa, and Europe. But the growth of European power led to an era during the 18th, 19th, and 20th centuries in which European states

The Kaaba, an ancient square building located in the Grand Mosque of Mecca, is considered by Muslims to be the holiest place in the world. Walking around this ancient shrine is an important part of the ritual Hajj pilgrimage.

established control over Muslim lands. As a result Muslims adapted differing viewpoints on the role of Islam in political and social life.

Some reformers argued that Muslims should not simply accept or reject Western ideals, but should reinterpret traditional Islamic institutions and law in order to adapt to the contemporary situation. A few believed that the only way to prosperity in the modern era was to fully Westernize, and to adopt secular modes of government and public life. These Muslims were known broadly as modernists.

Others began to call for a return to the roots of the Islamic faith as a way for Muslim societies to recover a sense of identity and reclaim power. These fundamentalists believe that Islamic political and cultural power declined because Muslims have strayed from the proper path of Islam. In their view, the only way to revitalize Muslim societies is to reestablish religious legal authority in every sphere of life. These Muslims have been widely referred to as Islamists, or Islamic fundamentalists, and their response to the pressures of modernity gained momentum during the early 20th century. Islamism is a sociopolitical movement that seeks to implement Sharia law wherever Muslims live. Islamist movements around the world are engaging in an ideological struggle against Western civilization and values. The most extremist groups promote jihad through the use of terrorism. Much of the time, Islamist ideology also contains an anti-

Sunnis and Shiites

Islam has two main branches: Sunnism and Shiism, or Shia. In some places there is considerable tension, and even hostility, between Sunnis and Shiites.

The rift between the Sunnis and the Shiites has its origins in the period after the death of Muhammad. While he was alive, Muhammad was the undisputed leader of the Muslim community. While no one could replace him as prophet—Muslims considered him God's last (and greatest) prophet—his death in 632 C.E. left the growing Muslim community in need of a spiritual and temporal leader, or caliph. The question was, how should the caliph be chosen? Many believed that the leading men in the Muslim community should select the caliph. These people came to be called Sunnis (the name *Sunni* comes from an Arabic word meaning "the path"— that is, the path Muhammad intended Muslims to follow). Others, however, believed that the position of caliph should be passed down through Muhammad's bloodline. Muhammad did not have a son who survived to adulthood; his closest male relative was Ali ibn Abi Talib, his cousin and son-in-law. Muslims who believed Ali should be caliph would eventually come to be known as Shiites (from *shiat Ali*, Arabic for "party of Ali").

Semitic strain. The scope and numbers of these Islamist groups have been increasing especially since the 1990s.

Islamists promote an interpretation of the Qur'an and Hadith that turns Islam into an often oppressive and violent religion. For example, while jihad is certainly a traditional concept, its understanding has changed. While at one time the term referred to a personal struggle to live a life infused with and guided by Islamic law and values, Islamists have reinterpreted the concept to mean the obligation of undertaking a physical struggle against all nonbelievers. Similarly, the Qur'an contains many statements regarding the Jews; in many eras throughout Islamic rule, Jews were

In the matter of selecting a caliph, the Sunni group prevailed. Abu Bakr, a close companion of Muhammad's, became the Prophet's first successor. Ali would ultimately be chosen as the fourth caliph. His tenure, however, was marred by dissension among Muslims, and Ali was murdered by members of a splinter group.

After Ali's death, Muawiya—the governor of Syria and a member of the Umayyad family, which had originally opposed Islam—consolidated power and installed himself as caliph. Departing from the practice of electing a caliph, Muawiya established a hereditary dynasty so that his son could succeed him as leader of the Muslims.

However, Ali's followers continued to insist that the caliph should follow his bloodline. Muawiya and his successors took steps to eliminate threats to their power. Despite the fact that he had renounced any claim to the caliphate, Ali's son Hassan was poisoned in 669 C.E. Ali's other son, Hussein, pressed his claim, however. In 680 Hussein and his followers were massacred by the forces of the Umayyad caliph Yazid at the Battle of Karbala.

Despite the deaths of these leaders, the Shiite sect survived. Today, Shiites make up about 14 percent of the world's Muslims; they form a majority in a few countries, such as Iran, Iraq, and Bahrain. Sunnis, meanwhile, constitute more than 80 percent of all Muslims worldwide.

Islamists seek to return the Muslim world to a so-called "golden age of Islam"—a period in the seventh century when Muhammad and his immediate successors (known as rashidun, or "rightly guided" caliphs) led the faithful. Although Islamists reject many aspects of the modern world, they are willing to use modern technology, such as cell phones, television, and the Internet, to accomplish their goals. This is the Web site of the Egyptian Islamist Yusuf al-Qaradawi.

given certain rights (though not equal to Muslims) as "people of the book," but Islamists have seized upon the most anti-Semitic statements in the Qur'an and have made anti-Semitism a central tenet of the ideology. While most Muslims may not identify with Islamism, not all Muslims identify with Islamism, but this fundamentalist movement is growing in prominence, scope, and followers throughout the world. Because of Islamist influences, conflicts in which Muslims attack non-Muslims have been proliferating.

An Islamist group called the Muslim Brotherhood took the lead in the Arab world. It was established in Egypt in 1928 by Hasan al-Banna (1906–1949), who used Islamic symbols to build greater unity among Egyptians in resistance to the British colonial presence and later developed extensive social programs for Egyptians living under independent but secular rule. The

Islamic Society of India, founded in 1941 by Mawlana Mawdudi (1903–1979), shared much the same approach.

Both al-Banna and Mawdudi influenced Sayyid Qutb (1906–1966), a prominent Egyptian member of the Muslim Brotherhood. In his books *In the Shade of the Qur'an*, a multivolume commentary on the Qur'an, and *Milestones,* Qutb provided an in-depth response to the tensions between Islam and the West. Qutb extended Mawdudi's assessment that Western societies were barbaric (jahiliyyah) because of their lack of Islamic rule. As the Egyptian government brutally suppressed the Muslim Brotherhood, he concluded that his own country's leaders were also jahiliyyah and must be forcibly removed from power. Qutb based his thinking in part on time he spent in the United States, where he was appalled by what he saw as unbridled materialism, sexual promiscuity, and racism. Although Qutb was eventually executed by the Egyptian government, his writings continue to exert a strong influence on Islamists today.

Another influential Islamist is Yusuf al-Qaradawi, who has written over 100 books and runs an Arabic-language Web site where he offers conservative interpretations of the Qur'an and boasts that every Muslim has been exposed to his work in some way. Referring to himself as a reformer, Qaradawi argues that Islam should adapt to the modern world based on past traditions. He is critical of the West, believing it to be morally corrupt for not adhering to Islam. He proffers anti-Semitic statements, calling for the destruction of the Jews and Israel and supporting suicide bombings.

Muslims in Asia and the Middle East

The Islamic world today is highly diverse, with Muslims in different places claiming different ethnic backgrounds and national identities, occupying a range of socioeconomic statuses, speaking different languages, and holding divergent attitudes toward the modern world. The remainder of this book briefly examines the state of Islam today, providing statistics on the Muslim populations of various countries and highlighting national and regional issues (including conflicts) involving Islam.

Muslims in Asia

Asia is the largest continent, covering 30 percent of the world's total land area. It is also the world's most populous continent, with nearly three-fifths of all people. In many parts of Asia, Islam is the dominant religion.

This mosque in Kuala Lumpur, the capital and largest city of Malaysia, blends distinctly Asian and Islamic architectural features. Historically, Islam as practiced in Asia has differed somewhat from Islam as practiced in the Middle East. In general, Asian Muslims have been less rigid in their beliefs and more tolerant of non-Islamic influences than Arab Muslims. In recent years, however, some Asian countries have seen a marked rise in Islamic fundamentalism—and at least part of this trend can be attributed to the influence of conservative Arab states such as Saudi Arabia.

With one exception (Kazakhstan), the countries of Central Asia all have populations that are overwhelmingly Muslim. About 99 percent of Afghanistan's 33.6 million people are Muslims. (Unless otherwise indicated, all population figures are 2009 estimates from the CIA World Factbook.) Islam is also the majority religion in four of the small Central Asian states that were once part of the Soviet Union. In the largest of these, Uzbekistan, 88 percent of the country's population of 27.6 million—or 24.2 million people—are Muslims. In Kyrgyzstan 75 percent of the approximately 5.4 million people are Muslim; 90 percent of Tajikistan's 7.3 million people are followers of

Islam, as are 89 percent of Turkmenistan's 4.8 million citizens. In Kazakhstan, another former Soviet state, Muslims constitute a plurality of the 15.3 million people (47 percent, compared with 44 percent Orthodox Christians).

South Asia contains countries with very large populations—and very large Muslim populations. Approximately 95 percent of Pakistan's 176 million people are adherents of Islam, giving Pakistan an estimated 167 million Muslims. That is more Muslims than live on the entire Arabian Peninsula. About 80.5 percent of India's people are Hindus, compared with just 13.4 percent Muslims. Yet because the country is so populous—it has more than 1.1 billion people—there are an estimated 155 million Indian Muslims. In Bangladesh, Muslims are the majority (83 percent) and Hindus the minority (16 percent). There are more than 129 million Muslims in Bangladesh.

Young Indonesian Muslims play together in a mosque. Indonesia is home to more Muslims than any other country; traders and missionaries originally brought the religion to the islands during the 13th century.

Islam had spread as far east as China by the eighth century, but there are fewer Muslims living in eastern Asia. China has a Muslim population of between 20 and 26 million. (This communist country is officially atheist.) There are also small Muslim communities in Japan, South Korea, Mongolia, and Nepal.

Southeast Asia is home to several countries in which a majority of the people are Muslims. These include Indonesia (the world's largest Muslim nation, with more than 205 million adherents of Islam), Malaysia, and Brunei. Almost 15 percent of Singapore's 4.6 million people follow Islam; most of these people are the ethnic Malays who live in the country. More than 80 percent of Filipinos are Catholic, but the Philippines has a Muslim population of about 4.8 million, approximately 5 percent of the country's total population. Burma (also called Myanmar), Vietnam, and Thailand are home to smaller communities of Muslims.

Religious Conflicts in Asia

Asia gave birth to some of the world's oldest civilizations, and today many Asians are followers of the ancient religions Hinduism and Buddhism. Asians practice a variety of other local religions, as well as Christianity. Against this backdrop of religious diversity, numerous conflicts involving Muslims have occurred over the years.

For example, the modern states of India and Pakistan were born amid terrible Hindu-Muslim violence in 1947, when British colonial rule in South Asia ended. Since then, India and Pakistan have continuously been at odds over the Kashmir region. India has controlled most of Kashmir since 1947, even though many Muslim Kashmiris would prefer to become part of Pakistan. The dispute over this territory continues to be a major source of tension in the region. India and Pakistan have gone to war several times over Kashmir, most recently in 1999. The consequences of a full-scale war could be grave, as both India and Pakistan have nuclear weapons.

Pakistan sponsors Islamist terrorists who attack Indian targets. Many of these attacks have taken place in Kashmir. In October 2001, for example, a Pakistan-based Kashmiri terrorist group called Jaish-e-Mohammed attacked the legislature of India's Jammu and Kashmir state in the summer capital of Srinagar. About 35 people were killed. The following year, an attack in the winter capital of Jammu claimed more than 30 lives. Other Islamist terror groups with links to Pakistan have struck deep inside India. One such attack, in December 2001, targeted India's Parliament in New Delhi; a dozen people were killed in the incident. A deadlier attack—or more precisely, a series of attacks—began on November 26, 2008, in Mumbai, India's financial capital. Terrorists linked to the Pakistan-based group Lashkar-e-Taiba attacked a rail station, two luxury hotels, and a hospital in Mumbai, among other targets. They killed more than 160 people.

Although Muslims were the perpetrators of these and many other terrorist attacks against India, their motivations were not expressly religious but political—namely, to compel India to relinquish control of Kashmir. India has also been rocked by large-scale violence that is directly attributable to religious resentments. And Muslims are just as often the victims as the perpetrators.

The animosity between India's majority Hindus and its minority Muslims goes back a millennium. A series of Muslim conquerors raided India after 1000 C.E., and the Muslim Mughal dynasty ruled India from the early 16th century until it was displaced by British imperialists, beginning in the 18th century.

In many ways, controversies surrounding the town of Ayodhya, in the Indian state of Uttar Pradesh, are emblematic of

U.N. peacekeepers examine a map while stationed on the Line of Control, a border between India and Pakistan that runs through the disputed Kashmir region, October 2005.

the Hindu-Muslim rift. Ayodhya was the site of the Babri Masjid, a Mughal-era mosque. Hindus consider Ayodhya the birthplace of Rama, and they long claimed that the Babri Masjid was built over an earlier temple to that important Hindu deity. In the early 1980s, militant Hindu groups began a campaign to have the Babri Masjid demolished and a temple to Rama constructed. In October 1990 approximately 20,000 Hindus stormed the mosque, triggering violence that claimed the lives of nearly 250 people. The Hindus were eventually expelled from the Babri Masjid. Two years later, however, an estimated 300,000 Hindus descended on the mosque and completely demolished it with shovels, crowbars, and axes. Nationwide rioting ensued, during which more than 2,000 people were killed.

A memorial to the more than 200 victims of an October 2002 terrorist attack in Bali, Indonesia. The attack was carried out by agents of Jemaah Islamiyah, an Islamist organization that wishes to establish a caliphate—a government controlled by Muslim religious leaders—to rule over Asia.

For years afterward, the status of the site was litigated in Indian courts. Tensions simmered, finally exploding into a rampage of deadly sectarian violence in early 2002. In February of that year, Hindus staged a large rally in Ayodhya. On the 27th, as several hundred of these demonstrators were returning to Ahmadabad, in the state of Gujarat, the train on which they were traveling was stopped and apparently set on fire by a mob of Muslims. Fifty-nine Hindus were killed. Almost immediately, Hindu mobs retaliated in Ahmadabad, burning Muslims' homes and businesses, raping Muslim women, and murdering Muslim men, women, and children. The carnage quickly spread throughout Gujarat. More than 2,000 people were killed, and at least 100,000 were driven from their homes, before the violence began to subside six weeks later. Most of the victims were Muslims.

But conflicts involving Muslims in Asia are not restricted to India and Pakistan. Jemaah Islamiyah (JI) is arguably the most dangerous and widespread Islamist organization in Southeast Asia. JI has close ties to Osama bin Laden's al-Qaeda organization, which sponsored the terrorist attacks against the United States of September 11, 2001. JI's goal is to create a caliphate, ruled by Islamic law, in the entire region spanning from Burma (Myanmar) in the west to the Philippines in the east. The group's members hope this Islamic state will in time become part of the larger caliphate that al-Qaeda envisions as governing the world-wide Muslim community. To accomplish this goal, Jemaah Islamiyah has attacked civilian targets. The most notable attacks were a car bombing in Bali, Indonesia, in 2002 that resulted in 202 civilian deaths; the bombing of the Australian embassy in Jakarta, Indonesia, in 2004; and a series of suicide bomb attacks in Bali during October 2005.

Many conflicts in the region involving Muslims are more localized. In the Philippines, the Muslim Moro people of southern Mindanao Island have fought for years with the Philippine government, arguing for greater freedom and for closer relations with the Muslims who live in Malaysia's state of Sabah. In 1996 the Philippine government and the largest rebel group reached an agreement to create an autonomous region for the Muslims. But through acts of terrorism the Moro Islamic Liberation Front (MILF) quickly destroyed that agreement—and supplanted Muslim nationalists. The MILF, which continues to fight the Philippine government, seeks to create an independent Muslim state.

In southern Thailand, an uprising among Muslim ethnic Malays—including bombings, beheadings, and shootings—has claimed more than 3,400 lives since 2004. The Malay insurgents want an Islamic state separate from predominantly Buddhist Thailand.

The Middle East

Most of the countries in the region historically known as the Middle East—the Arabian Peninsula and eastern Mediterranean—have an Arab majority. (There is no precise definition of the Middle East, though typically Egypt, in northeastern Africa, is included; for purposes of this volume, however, Egypt is included in the chapter on Africa.) People in the Middle East are also overwhelmingly Muslim. About 97 percent of Iraq's 28.9 million people follow Islam, as do virtually all of Saudi Arabia's 28.6 million people. In Yemen, well over 95 percent of the 23 million inhabitants are Muslims; in Syria, whose population is about 20 million, approximately 90 percent of the people follow Islam. Some 92 percent of Jordan's 6.3 million people are Muslims. Smaller Arab countries of

Mahmoud Ahmadinejad, president of the Islamic Republic of Iran, speaks before the United Nations. Iran, the most populous country of the Middle East, has been ruled by Shiite Islamic clerics since 1979. Today, Western observers are concerned about Iran's program to develop nuclear weapons, as well as the country's sponsorship of terrorist groups like Hezbollah.

the Middle East where the proportion of Muslims in the population is at least 90 percent include Oman, Kuwait, the United Arab Emirates, Bahrain, and Qatar. In Lebanon, home to about 4 million people, nearly 6 in 10 are Muslims (with almost all of the remainder belonging to a Christian denomination).

Iran is home to more than 66 million people. Ethnically, however, Iran is predominantly Persian rather than Arab. Still, an estimated 98 percent of Iranians follow Islam.

The Jewish state of Israel is the only country in the entire Middle East that does not have a majority Muslim population. There are about 7.2 million people living in Israel; about 76 percent are Jewish, while about 16 percent are Muslim. (Israel also has a small Christian population composed mainly of Christian Arabs.)

Conflict in the Middle East

Since the founding of Israel in May 1948, the Jewish state and its Muslim Arab neighbors have fought three major wars and several smaller ones. In addition, Israel has faced continual terrorist violence—some of it perpetrated by Palestinian nationalist groups like Fatah, and much of it by groups like Hamas and Hezbollah, which promote the complete elimination of Israel, a tenet that is central to Islamism. The Israeli response to terrorism has typically been quite forceful.

The reality, however, is that much strife in the Middle East is unrelated to the Arab-Israeli conflict in general or the Palestinian cause in particular. The Middle East's countries may be overwhelmingly Muslim, but that shared religious identity masks deep sectarian divisions. In Saudi Arabia, for example, a puritanical form of Sunni Islam known in the West as Wahhabism is the official religion, and the country's Shia are repressed. Elsewhere, the political ambitions of national leaders frequently trump religion.

The tragic consequences of a leader's unrestrained ambitions and of sectarian divisions can both be seen in the recent history of Iraq. In September 1980 Saddam Hussein, Iraq's dictator, ordered the invasion of neighboring Iran. The two countries had a long history of antagonism. Culture was one major factor (Iraq is Arab; Iran is Persian). Religious differences were another. While Shia Muslims constitute a majority in both countries (nearly 90 percent in Iran, about 60 percent in Iraq), Iraq's Sunni minority held power, though Saddam Hussein's regime was actually secular. In Iran a revolution had overthrown the regime of the secular-oriented, pro-Western Shah Mohammad Reza Pahlavi in early 1979. After the shah's downfall, hard-line Islamist Shiites led by the Ayatollah Ruhollah Khomeini took power in Tehran. Khomeini soon began stirring up opposition to Saddam Hussein among Iraq's Shiites. Saddam, seeing continuing disorder in Iranian society, believed his neighbor militarily vulnerable and eyed Iran's oil-rich—and largely Arab—province of Khuzestan.

Saddam's decision to invade Iran provoked a bloody, eight-year-long war. After initial gains by the Iraqi armed forces, the Iranians successfully counterattacked. The war settled into a brutal stalemate, with total casualties exceeding a million before the fighting finally ended in 1988.

Iraq had borrowed heavily from oil-producing Arab Gulf States such as Kuwait and Saudi Arabia in order to finance the long war. Now, with the war over and his country's economy in shambles, Saddam asked the Gulf States to forgive Iraq's debts. After all, Saddam argued, Iraq had protected the Gulf States against any Iranian attempts to export its Islamic revolution (or Shia or Persian influence generally) into those countries. Iraq's creditors were unmoved by this argument, infuriating Saddam. The dictator ordered his armed forces to invade Kuwait in August 1990—a play for power that would have enriched Iraq, given it control over approximately 40 percent of the world's oil, and made it the de facto leader of the Arab world.

The United Nations condemned the invasion and demanded that Iraqi forces withdraw from Kuwait. Saddam Hussein refused. The UN authorized member states to expel the Iraqis forcibly from Kuwait. In early 1991, in the Gulf War, an international coalition led by the United States routed Iraq but left Saddam in power. Still, his days appeared numbered, and in the wake of the March 3 Gulf War cease-fire, rebellions against the Iraqi dictator broke out. In the southern part of the country, Iraqi Shiites rose up. In the north, Saddam faced an uprising from Kurds, who are Sunni Muslims but not Arabs. Saddam's forces brutally suppressed both uprisings.

Iraq's dictator, Saddam Hussein, waged a long and bloody war against neighboring Iran (1980-1988). During that time he brutally suppressed Iraq's Shiites and Kurds, two groups he saw as threats to his power. In 1990, angered at Kuwait's refusal to forgive debts incurred during the Iran-Iraq War, Saddam sent his army to conquer the tiny emirate.

After the al-Qaeda terrorist attacks of September 11, 2001, the administration of U.S. president George W. Bush made the case for an invasion of Iraq, alleging that Iraq had failed to fully dismantle its nuclear-, chemical-, and biological-weapons programs—a requirement imposed by the armistice agreement that ended the Gulf War—and that Iraq had links to al-Qaeda. Administration officials reassured Americans that removing Saddam and creating a stable and democratic Iraq would be relatively easy. Many things went wrong in the aftermath of the March 2003 U.S. invasion. Clearly, however, a major problem

An Israeli airstrike destroys an enemy target in the Gaza Strip. The Palestinian terrorist organization Hamas, which has sworn to destroy the state of Israel, has controlled Gaza since 2007. Hamas operatives regularly launch rocket attacks against settlements within Israel.

that the Bush administration had failed to anticipate was the hostility between Iraq's Sunni Arab and Shiite communities. Sectarian bloodletting would wrack Iraq for years and claim tens of thousands of lives.

Sectarian divisions also fueled a long civil war in Lebanon (1975–1990). Broadly speaking, the fighting began with several major groups of combatants: Christians, Sunni Muslims, Druze, and Palestinians. But multiple factions existed within each of these groups—for example, among the Muslims there were Sunni and Shia militias—and the factions sometimes turned on each other. Alliances shifted as each group vied for political control of the country. Further complicating the situation, Syrian troops seized control of Lebanon in 1976, under the guise of restoring order, and Israel launched two invasions, in 1978 and 1982, to stop cross-border terrorism from Palestinian groups. After the 1982 invasion, the Shia Islamist organization Hezbollah ("Party of God") was formed to fight Israeli forces in Lebanon and to increase the power of the Shia community.

Israeli forces withdrew from Lebanon in 2000, but Hezbollah—which is supported by Iran and Syria—continued to mount attacks against Israel. In July of 2006, Hezbollah fighters slipped into northern Israel from Lebanon and attacked an Israeli army patrol. This sparked a month-long war between Israel and Hezbollah, during which Israeli forces tried to wipe out Hezbollah, which was showering the north of Israel with missiles. The majority of the people killed were Lebanese civilians.

Although Hezbollah is a Shiite organization, it has cooperated with the militant Palestinian group Hamas, which is Sunni. Both groups adhere to a similar Islamist ideology that calls for the total annihilation of Israel. While Hamas is a political party and provides social services for Palestinians, it is also a terrorist organization. The Hamas charter calls for an Islamist state in all of Palestine and proclaims the desire to obliterate Israel. Like Hezbollah, Hamas has regularly attacked Israeli military and civilian targets in the West Bank, the Gaza Strip, and Israel proper. In June 2007, Hamas effectively took control of the Gaza Strip, a move that resulted in international condemnation. The group's continual firing of rockets into Israel provoked an Israeli invasion of Gaza in early 2009.

Another country struggling with Islamic extremism is Afghanistan. In late 1979, Soviet troops invaded Afghanistan to prop up a Communist regime that had seized power there. During most of the 1980s, the Soviets battled Afghan guerrillas and Muslim fighters from other countries who came to their aid. In the aftermath of the Soviet pullout in 1989, Afghanistan suffered years of continued violence as regional warlords vied for power. By 1996 a Pakistan-supported militia known as the Taliban had gained control over the capital, Kabul, as well as much of the country. The Taliban instituted a draconian form of Sharia (an Islamic legal system based on the Qur'an and other sources). Women were forbidden to leave their homes unaccompanied by a male relative, and when they did go out in public they were forced to completely cover their faces and bodies with a head-to-toe garment known as the burka. The Taliban also outlawed education for girls and prohibited women from working; banned music, television, and movies; amputated the hands of thieves; and carried out many public executions. The Taliban gave sanctuary to Osama bin Laden and his al-Qaeda terrorist organization, and after the 2001 al-Qaeda attacks on the United States, a U.S.-led coalition invaded Afghanistan and toppled the Taliban. In 2004 Hamid Karzai became Afghanistan's first democratically elected president, but his government was unable to consolidate its control throughout the country. By the summer of 2009, a resurgent Taliban threatened the Afghan government. The Taliban is also a major concern in neighboring Pakistan. Though Pakistan had formerly been a main sponsor of the group, by 2009 Pakistani troops were fighting the Taliban for control of the Swat Valley.

The United States has supported Hamid Karzai, the democratically elected president of Afghanistan, in his effort to prevent the Islamist Taliban from seizing power in the war-torn country.

Muslims in Europe

The great majority of Europe's people are Christians, and Roman Catholics form the single largest religious group in the region. However, the number of Muslims in Europe is growing. Recent estimates put the Muslim population of Europe at more than 50 million, out of a total European population of some 730 million.

Arguably the most difficult issue facing Europe's Muslim minorities has been whether—and to what extent—to assimilate into the societies in which they live. For many Muslims, the largely secular outlook of European societies is incompatible with Islamic values.

Muslims in Western and Central Europe

Although Muslims represent only a small percentage of the total population of Western Europe, they may be found in fairly large

Muslim Moors built the Alhambra, a famous fortress in Granada, Spain, in the 14th century. Muslim armies had invaded the Iberian Peninsula in 711 and soon conquered a large area, which they called al-Andalus. The kingdom of al-Andalus survived until 1492, when Spanish Christians regained control of the region after hundreds of years of fighting.

numbers in France, Germany, and the United Kingdom. Each of these European countries controlled colonies in the Islamic world during the 19th and early 20th centuries, and they permitted Muslims to immigrate.

France, for example, ruled large parts of North Africa during the 19th century and the first half of the 20th century. Algeria, one of the largest countries in Africa, won its freedom from French rule in 1961 after a bloody eight-year-long war for independence. However, Algeria underwent its own devastating civil war during the 1990s, and many Algerian Muslims immigrated to France to escape the violence. Today, France has a Muslim community numbered at 4 million to 5 million people.

Britain's Muslim population, which today stands at more than a million, can be traced in part to its long involvement in the Middle East and Asia. Many Muslim Indians, Pakistanis, and Arabs are drawn to the United Kingdom by its educational opportunities.

Many of the Muslims living in Germany today are immigrants from Turkey. Though it has a strong manufacturing base, Germany has suffered shortages of workers, and Turkish Muslims have seen an opportunity to take good-paying jobs. Today, the Muslim population of Germany is estimated at more than 3 million, or about 3.7 percent of Europe's most populous country.

Even countries in which the Roman Catholic Church has a very strong presence, such as Spain and Italy, are attracting Muslim immigrants. It is estimated that there are Muslim communities of between 500,000 and 800,000 people in each of those countries. There are also significant Muslim communities in Sweden, Belgium, Denmark, Norway, and the Netherlands. And the official statistics do not take into account undocumented, or illegal, Muslim immigrants to these countries.

Muslims in Eastern Europe

Russia, which straddles both Asia and Europe, has a large Muslim population. In fact, with more than 20 million believers, Islam is second only to the Orthodox Christian Church as the country's largest religious group. Most Russian Muslims are found in the republics of Tatarstan and Bashkortostan in the middle Volga region, and in the republics of Chechnya, Ingushetia, Alania (North Ossetia), Kabardino-Balkaria, and Dagestan. More than 95 percent of Russian Muslims are Sunnis. In 2005 the Russian government was admitted as an observer state to the Organization of the Islamic Conference (OIC).

Turkey, which is also located both in Europe and in Asia, claims the largest Muslim population in Europe, with more than

76 million followers of Islam. The modern state of Turkey was founded in 1923 out of the ruins of the Ottoman Empire. From the beginning, nationalist leaders like Kemal Atatürk established the government on a firmly secular basis. This policy of secularism has resulted in problems. Although many residents of Turkey seem to prefer the separation of mosque and state, some Islamists argue that Islamic laws and values should play a much greater role in the government's operation. And since 2002, the AK Party—which has roots in political Islam and has at times skirted Turkey's laws against religion in government—has been in power in Turkey.

Islam in southeastern Europe is in part a legacy of Ottoman rule over this region, which lasted from the 16th through the early 20th centuries. On the Balkan Peninsula, located to the north and west of Turkey, many countries have significant Muslim populations. One of these is Albania, where it is estimated that about 70 percent of the country's 3.6 million residents are Muslims. Although the practice of Islam was outlawed in Albania for many years by the country's Communist government, since the early 1990s Muslims have been permitted to worship freely. Today, according to the Albanian government, there are more than 1,000 mosques in the country.

Several countries that were once part of Yugoslavia have large Muslim populations. In Kosovo, an ethnic Albanian enclave that declared its independence from the former Yugoslav republic of Serbia in 2008, about 90 percent of the country's 2 million residents are Muslims. Muslims account for about 40 percent of the 4.6 million citizens of Bosnia and Herzegovina, and about 33 percent of the former Yugoslav republics of Macedonia and Montenegro.

Other countries in the Balkan region that have significant Muslim populations include Bulgaria, where about 12 percent of the country's 7.2 million people follow Islam; and Serbia, where Muslims make up 3.2 percent of that country's 7.4 million residents.

Conflicts in Europe

During the 1990s, the Balkan Peninsula was the site of bloody fighting fueled, at least in part, by animosity between Muslims and Christians. The breakup of Yugoslavia led to a decade of fighting in the region. After Bosnia and Herzegovina declared its independence in 1992, a brutal, ethnically based civil war raged there for three years. The conflict claimed nearly 250,000 lives, and about a million people were driven from their homes. Most were Bosnian Muslims, more than 30,000 of whom came to the United States as refugees. Later in the decade, fighting in Kosovo displaced some 900,000 people. To prevent a humanitarian disaster, the United States agreed to accept 20,000 Kosovar refugees. Other nations took in displaced Kosovars as well.

Bosnian Muslims (or Bosniaks) pass through a checkpoint manned by UN peacekeepers near Stari Vitez, May 1994.

The Russian government has also faced conflict involving its Muslim population. In Chechnya, a republic of Russia in the northern Caucasus Mountains, Muslim rebel groups began a war for independence in 1994. Although an uneasy peace agreement was signed after two years of fighting, the conflict erupted again in the late 1990s. Today, Russia maintains a strong military presence in Chechnya, but guerrilla fighting and terrorist-style attacks continue.

Other European countries have also faced terrorist attacks from Muslim extremists. In November 2003, al-Qaeda operatives detonated a series of truck bombs in Istanbul, Turkey, killing 57 people and injuring more than 700. On March 11, 2004, bombings on commuter trains in Madrid, Spain, killed nearly 200 people. The attacks—believed to have been committed by extremists inspired by al-Qaeda—may have contributed to the defeat of the Spanish political party in power in elections held three days later. That party, the Partido Popular, had supported the Bush administration's 2003 decision to invade Iraq and had sent Spanish troops to assist in the effort to remove Saddam Hussein from power.

A similar attack occurred in London on July 7, 2005, when British Muslim extremists carried out a series of suicide bombings on the city's public transportation system. The bombings killed more than 50 people and injured over 700. Many people believe the attacks were inspired by British military involvement in Iraq and Afghanistan.

Contemporary Issues in Western Europe

In Western Europe, most people believe that religious considerations should be excluded from political and civic affairs, regardless of whether a country's citizens are religious or secular in their personal lives. In many Western European countries, the liberal tradition of separation of church and state has in recent years come up against an Islamist ideology—embraced by some Muslim immigrants and their children—that seeks to change European society to conform to Islam.

In 2005, for example, the Danish newspaper *Jyllands-Posten* published 12 editorial cartoons that depicted the prophet Muhammad and the Islamic religion in an unflattering light. This led to protests by Danish Muslims, and an outcry from leaders in the Muslim world. The cartoons inflamed a debate over freedom of speech in Europe. Defenders of the newspaper said that it is legitimate to criticize or poke fun at any religion. Critics felt the newspaper was simply trying to provoke a controversy by publishing cartoons offensive to Muslims.

In recent years, young Muslims in Europe have tried to assert their religious ideology by dressing in traditional clothing worn elsewhere in the Islamic world, such as cloaks (*abaya*) and headscarves (*hijab*). The Qur'an does not stipulate that women must cover themselves entirely, but this practice follows the trend in fundamental Islamist interpretations of the religion. While some women claim that dressing in such a way allows them to express their identity as devout Muslims, others feel that doing so is not mandated by normative Muslim law. In France, the government passed a law in 2004 that prohibited Muslim girls from wearing headscarves to public schools, in line with the secular government's stance banning the display of overt religious symbols in schools. Bans on veils and headscarves have also been debated in other countries, including the United Kingdom, Germany, and the Netherlands. Countries like Denmark and Sweden, on the other hand, have not prevented Muslims from wearing the *hijab*, *abaya*, or *burka*, as mandated by some religious leaders.

In some countries, including Sweden and the United Kingdom, Muslim groups have asked the governments to establish courts that would use Sharia, or Islamic law, in cases involving family or civil law, such as divorces, financial disputes, and other matters. In the United Kingdom, some informal Sharia tribunals are currently operating in London and several other cities. However, all parties involved in a dispute must agree to use the Sharia court and abide by its decision, rather than having their case heard in a British court. Also, the British government has said that Sharia court rulings may not violate English law or public policy. Still, some people have raised concerns about cases in which liberal values might clash with Islamic ones—particularly regarding women, as men are favored under Islamic law.

The May 2007 election of Nicolas Sarkozy as France's president triggered riots in the streets of Paris. Sarkozy had earlier angered French Muslims with comments they perceived as offensive—including his observation that Muslims in France should be obligated to respect the country's laws, to refrain from oppressing girls or taking more than one wife, and to stop slaughtering sheep at their homes.

Muslims in Africa

The African continent is home to the second-largest population of Muslims in the world. There are an estimated 400 million followers of Islam living in Africa. Only Asia has a larger Muslim population.

In North Africa, which includes Egypt, Algeria, Libya, Morocco, and Tunisia, most of the people are Muslims, and Islam is both the state religion and an integral part of social life. Additionally, every country of sub-Saharan Africa also contains a Muslim community.

Islam was brought to North Africa by conquering armies of Arab Muslims in the seventh century. However, the religion spread through the rest of the continent in a centuries-long process of diffusion, with the help of Muslim merchants and missionaries who brought the message of Muhammad along the trade routes. Historically, North African cities like Cairo (home

A group of Muslims pray in the desert, Morocco. The North African states are home to about half of Africa's Muslim population.

of al-Azhar University), Tlemcen (in Algeria), and Fez (in Morocco) served as important centers of Islamic thought. These were places where important religious issues were developed and debated. The development of Islam in sub-Saharan Africa was less pronounced, though Timbuktu in modern-day Mali was a major center of Islamic learning in the 15th century. Since then, Islam has taken hold throughout West Africa, though in many ways it has been adapted and infused with influences from local cultures.

The Distribution of Muslims in Africa

Approximately half of the continent's 400 million Muslims live in the North African states. These include Egypt (72 million), Algeria (32.5 million), Morocco (31.3 million), Tunisia (9.7 million), Libya (5.4 million), Mauritania (2.9 million), and the disputed Western Sahara territory (about 260,000). Overall in North Africa, more than 95 percent of the population adheres to Islam.

The number of Muslims in sub-Saharan Africa is growing rapidly. The largest concentration of Muslims living south of the Sahara can be found in Nigeria, where about half of the country's total population of 133 million people are Muslims. Other West African countries also have significant Muslim populations. More than 80 percent of the population is Muslim in Mali (10.4 million), Senegal (9.9 million), Niger (8.8 million), Guinea (7.7 million), and The Gambia (1.4 million). Muslims are a majority in Burkina Faso (6.7 million) and Sierra Leone (3.4 million). There are also Muslim communities of significant size in Benin, Cote d'Ivoire, Ghana, Liberia, and Togo.

Many countries of East Africa have significant Muslim populations, including Ethiopia (33 million), Tanzania (12.6 million), Somalia (more than 8 million), and Uganda (4.1 million). The Muslim population of Kenya is not known for certain; estimates range from 3.2 million to nearly 8 million. Other East African

Muslim women walk down a beach on the island of Zanzibar. Most people living on Tanzania—which since 1964 has been part of the East African state of Tanzania—follow Islam.

The Great Mosque of Djenne, a small city in central Mali, is the largest mud brick building in the world. Another city in Mali, Timbuktu, was an important center of Islamic scholarship during the 15th and 16th centuries.

countries with large Muslim communities are Malawi (2.3 million), Eritrea (2.2 million), Madagascar (1.2 million), and Djibouti (432,000).

In central Africa, Chad has a large Muslim community of over 4.7 million, more than half of the country's total population. Other countries of central Africa that have significant Muslim communities include the Democratic Republic of the Congo (5.6 million), Cameroon (3.15 million), the Central African Republic (550,000), and Rwanda (360,000).

In southern Africa, Zambia is home to about 2.4 million Muslims, or nearly a quarter of that country's total population. The proportion of Muslims in South Africa—the region's most populous nation, with 49 million people—is less than 2 percent. However, South African Muslims are well represented in government and have some influence in social affairs.

Contemporary Issues

Today, the daily practices of African Muslims vary greatly across the continent, depending on where they live. For example, in pre-dominantly Islamic North Africa, Muslims are given preferential treatment over non-Muslims in employment, in the legal system, and in government programs. In other countries where Muslims are not in the majority, they often live under secular government systems. There has been friction in countries like Kenya, where Muslim schoolgirls have sometimes been prohibited from wear-ing headscarves in class, and in Ethiopia, where despite the fact that Muslims make up nearly one-third of the population, they were for decades denied the right to own land, observe religious holidays, hold government jobs, and serve in the army.

Another source of conflict involving African Muslims is the way in which different African societies have chosen to interpret *Sharia* when using it as a basis for national or regional laws. In some countries *Sharia* is loosely interpreted, giving Muslims many personal freedoms, while in other countries a very conser-vative interpretation of *Sharia* is enforced. In such places, women have few rights and criminals are punished with particularly harsh sentences. Criminal sentences handed down by *Sharia* courts include the amputation of limbs (a thief's hand may be cut off, for example) or the execution of those convicted of adultery (often by stoning or hanging). When non-Muslims have been forced to live under *Sharia*, as in Nigeria and Sudan, violence has often erupted. A prominent example is the case of Sudan, which was decimated by a two-decade-long civil war caused in part by the Islamist government's attempts to impose Sharia law on non-Muslim Sudanese in the southern part of the country. In the 1990s, Sudan was host to Osama bin Laden, who built up terror-ist-training and financial networks from that country.

Muslims in the Americas

In the centuries after Christopher Columbus's 1492 voyage to the New World, immigrants from all over the globe settled in North and South America. It is not surprising, then, that Muslim communities in North and South America are also racially and ethnically very diverse. They are also ideologically diverse.

In the United States, the most populous country in the Western Hemisphere, Muslims make up a very small minority. The U.S. census does not collect data on religious affiliation, so it is difficult to say with precision how many Muslims live in the United States. But recent estimates put the number at between 2 million and 6 million, or about 1 to 2 percent of the total population.

To the north of the United States, Canada is home to about 783,700 Muslims, according to the country's 2006 census. That is about 2.5 percent of the country's population. To the south,

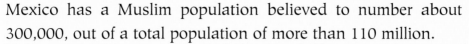

Mexico has a Muslim population believed to number about 300,000, out of a total population of more than 110 million.

Roman Catholicism remains the dominant religion of Latin America, but in recent decades the practice of Islam has grown more common in several South American and Caribbean countries. In South America, there are significant communities of believers in Suriname (about 93,000, or 19 percent of the population) and in Guyana (about 57,000, or 7.2 percent of the population). In the Caribbean state of Trinidad and Tobago, there are nearly 61,000 Muslims, about 5.8 percent of the population.

The American flag flies outside an Islamic center in Toledo, Ohio. In 2007, the Pew Research Center reported that the Muslim population of the United States is about 2.35 million.

A woman examines a display at the Arab American National Museum in Dearborn, Michigan. According to the Pew Research Center's 2007 study, about two-thirds (65 percent) of adult Muslim Americans were born in another country. Most of these immigrants came from the Arab states, Pakistan or other countries in South Asia, or from Iran.

The First Muslims in America

Between the 16th and 19th centuries, an estimated 10 million black Africans were brought against their will to the Western Hemisphere, where they were sold as slaves. Some 600,000 to 650,000 ended up in the British North American colonies. Scholars believe that perhaps 7 to 10 percent of these slaves were Muslims.

The first identifiable wave of Muslim immigrants to the United States arrived between 1875 and 1912. They were mostly Syrian, Lebanese, and Palestinian Arabs living under Ottoman rule; Arab Christians also emigrated from the deteriorating Ottoman Empire. Most of these immigrants were young, uneducated men who found jobs as peddlers or factory workers.

Many of the early Arab immigrants, both Christians and Muslims, settled in Detroit, Chicago, and other industrial cities of the Midwest. There small Muslim communities had developed by the second decade of the 20th century. (A group of Lebanese immigrants is generally credited with constructing the first building in the United States specifically designed as a mosque, in Ross, North Dakota, in 1929.)

A second wave of Muslim immigration to the United States began after World War I (1914–1918). Once again, the majority of the Muslim immigrants were Arabs who had lived under Ottoman rule before the empire was dismantled. However, legislation passed in the United States during the 1920s imposed limits on immigration. These laws had the effect of keeping out most people from the Muslim world.

Increasing Number of Immigrants

Immigration patterns shifted after World War II. Between 1947 and 1960, fewer people came from the Arab world. But the number of Muslims coming from Europe—especially Yugoslavia, Albania, and the Ukraine—increased. They were joined by a significant number of Muslims from India, where independence from Great Britain in 1947 was accompanied by a wave of Hindu-Muslim violence and the partition of the Subcontinent into predominantly Hindu India and predominantly Muslim Pakistan. Many of the Muslim immigrants from India were well educated and familiar with Western culture. Educational opportunities in the United States were a major attraction for this group, along with refuge from violence and from religious or social discrimination.

In 1965, President Lyndon B. Johnson signed the Immigration and Nationality Act into law. This legislation removed immigration restrictions based on national origin, allowing Muslim immigration to increase. In addition to more Arabs, Indians, and Europeans, Muslims from Southeast Asia, Iran, Pakistan, and Africa also began coming to the United States in significant numbers.

The Muslim immigrants and refugees who have come to the United States are quite diverse—not only ethnically and culturally, but also in the Islamic beliefs and traditions they hold.

The Nation of Islam

One uniquely American organization influenced by Islam is the Nation of Islam, which was established in the 1930s. The Nation of Islam adopted many aspects of Muslim culture and practice, including prayer, almsgiving, dietary restrictions, and even Arabic names. Yet many of its core teachings and values are opposed to those of normative Islam. For example, one of the group's early leaders, Elijah Muhammad, claimed that he was a prophet and that Wallace D. Fard, the Nation's founder, was God. Elijah Muhammad called white men "devils" and claimed that blacks are a superior race destined to rule the earth, contradicting the Islamic belief in the equality of all people before Allah.

The controversial Minister Louis Farrakhan has been the leader of the Nation of Islam since 1978. He has attracted many African-American converts with his commanding presence, soaring oratory, and powerful message of black self-improvement and self-reliance. In 1995 Farrakhan drew hundreds of thousands of African Americans from across the United States to the "Million Man March" in Washington, D.C. That event was essentially a call for African-American men to accept responsibility for their actions and to commit themselves to improving the black community.

However, many Americans consider Farrakhan a divisive figure, even a racist. And despite Farrakhan's periodic overtures to the worldwide Muslim community, most orthodox Muslims insist that the Nation of Islam is not an Islamic movement. They point to its continued exclusion of non-blacks, as well as various other teachings that are opposed to the Islam of the Qur'an.

Of the 35 percent of Muslims born in the United States, more than half are African-Americans.

Sunnis make up the largest proportion of the overall American Muslim population. They also represent the widest scope of ethnicities—coming from the Middle East, Central Asia, Southeast Asia, Europe, and Africa. Most converts to Islam in the United States are also Sunnis. The majority of Shiites—who constitute an estimated one-fifth of the U.S. Muslim population—come from Iran, Iraq, Pakistan, Afghanistan, and India. Still others are from offshoots of mainstream Islam, like the Sufis, Druze, and Ahmadiyya. As the Muslim community in the United States develops, this diversity plays an important role.

American Converts to Islam

Converts add to the rich mosaic of American Islam. Almost half of American Muslims are believed to be converts, and these converts are overwhelmingly African American. However, Islam appeals to individuals from many different social, racial, and economic groups.

African-American Muslim organizations have taken the lead in setting up programs to educate inmates in American prisons about Islam. It has been estimated that more than 300,000 prisoners are converts to Islam. Most of these prisoners are African Americans. However, Hispanics and Native Americans make up a proportion of the estimated 30,000 inmates who convert to Islam annually. Islam—with its emphasis on discipline, good conduct, and reform—holds great appeal for many who have run into trouble with the law.

Chronology

c.570: Muhammad is born on the Arabian Peninsula.

610: Muhammad receives the first revelation from Allah in a cave at Mount Hira.

622: Muhammad and his followers are forced to leave Mecca and move to Yathrib, an oasis town that is later renamed Medina.

630: Muhammad and his followers capture Mecca.

632: Muhammad dies; Abu Bakr becomes the first caliph.

661: The fourth caliph Ali is assassinated by disgruntled followers, ending the rule of the "rightly guided" caliphs and beginning the Umayyad dynasty of caliphs.

711: Muslim Moors conquer Spain.

717: Muslims attempt to conquer Constantinople.

750: The first of the four major Islamic schools of law are established; the Abbasid dynasty seizes power from the Umayyads.

1258: The Mongols sack Baghdad, ending the Abbasid's reign.

1453: The Ottoman Turks conquer Constantinople, bringing the Byzantine Empire to an end.

1511: A Portuguese army captures Malacca and establishes Portugal's dominance over the Indian Ocean.

1529: An Ottoman army besieges Vienna, but fails to capture the city.

1703: The Ottoman sultan Ahmed III begins a cultural revival.

1798: A French army under Napoleon conquers Egypt.

1830: France sends a military expedition against Algiers, capturing it and making Algeria a colony of France.

1919: The former Middle Eastern territories of the Ottoman Empire are divided among the victorious European allies after World War I.

1928: Hasan al-Banna founds the Muslim Brotherhood in Egypt.

1947: Great Britain grants independence to its colony in India, partitioning it into two states, India and Pakistan.

1953: The foundation stone is laid to enlarge the Prophet's Mosque in Medina.

1971: East Pakistan splits from Pakistan to form the country of Bangladesh.

1990: Iraq invades and annexes Kuwait, an aggressive move that is reversed the next year by a U.S.-led international coalition in the Gulf War.

1995: In July, 7,000 Bosnian Muslims are executed at Srebrenica by Bosnian Serbs, as part of a three-year program of genocide euphemistically called "ethnic cleansing."

2001: Two commercial airliners strike the World Trade Center complex in New York City, a third jet strikes the Pentagon outside Washington, D.C., and a fourth jet crashes into an open field in western Pennsylvania; the attacks are the work of Muslim extremists associated with the terrorist group al-Qaeda. A U.S.-led coalition invades Afghanistan and topples the Taliban regime, which had been sheltering al-Qaeda.

2003: The United States invades Iraq and topples the regime of Saddam Hussein; the war and subsequent occupation of Iraq stirs up angry anti-American feelings throughout the Islamic world.

2005: On July 7, Muslim extremists set off a series of bombs on London's public transportation system, killing more than 50 people and injuring over 700.

2008: The United Nations Security Council adopts Resolution 1803, which requires Iran to stop all programs to enrich uranium that could be used for atomic weapons.

2009: The worldwide Muslim population is estimated at 1.3 billion.

Glossary

adherent—someone who follows or supports a particular religion or cause.

atheist—a person who does not believe in God or deities.

autonomous region—an area within a nation-state that is politically independent and self-governing with regard to internal matters.

caliphate—an Islamic state ruled by a caliph (a Muslim spiritual and temporal leader).

companion—a good friend; in Islamic history, this term is used to refer to Muhammad's closest and most trusted followers.

diffusion—the spread of practices or beliefs from one culture to another.

doctrine—a body of ideas, particularly in religion, taught to people as truthful or correct.

Islamism—a fundamentalist Islamic political ideology that seeks to return Muslim societies to an earlier, supposed golden age in the history of Islam, with compulsory adherence to Sharia. Islamists support strict adherence to a literal interpretation of Islamic doctrine, accompanied by the elimination of modern influences or interpretation on the way Islam is practiced.

missionaries—people who are sent to spread religious beliefs to another area or country.

monotheism—the belief that there is only one God. Judaism, Christianity, and Islam are all considered monotheistic religions.

mosque—an Islamic house of worship.

polytheism—a religion in which multiple deities are worshipped.

al-Qaeda—an international Islamist terror organization established in Afghanistan in 1989; led by Osama bin Laden, it orchestrated the attacks of September 11, 2001, as well as many others against U.S. and other targets.

secularism—the belief that religious leaders and considerations should not influence political or civic affairs.

socioeconomic—relating to or involving a combination of social and economic factors.

umma—the worldwide community of Muslims, which is believed to transcend tribal and national boundaries.

Further Reading

Ayoob, Mohammed. *The Many Faces of Political Islam: Religion and Politics in the Muslim World*. Ann Arbor: University of Michigan Press, 2007.

Carr, Melissa S. *Who Are the Muslims?: Where Muslims Live and How They Are Governed*. Philadelphia: Mason Crest, 2004.

Esposito, John L., and Dalia Mogahed. *Who Speaks for Islam? What a Billion Muslims Really Think*. New York: Gallup Press, 2007.

Kennedy, Hugh. *The Great Arab Conquests: How the Spread of Islam Changed the World We Live In*. New York: Da Capo Press, 2007.

Kramer, Martin. *Arab Awakening and Islamic Revival: The Politics of Ideas in the Middle East*. Edison, N.J.: Transaction Publishers, 2008.

Lewis, Bernard, and Buntzie Ellis Churchill. *Islam: The Religion and the People*. Philadelphia: Wharton School Publishing, 2007.

Long, David E., et al. *The Government and Politics of the Middle East and North Africa*. 5th edition. Boulder, Colo.: Westview Press, 2007.

Rubin, Barry, ed. *Guide to Islamist Movements*. Armonk, N.Y.: M.E. Sharpe, 2009.

Internet Resources

http://www.oic-oci.org

Official Web site of the Organization of the Islamic Conference, an international organization of Muslim states.

http://www.pbs.org/empires/islam

The companion Web site to the PBS special "Islam: Empire of Faith" provides some history about the origins of Islam, its spread throughout the world, and key figures in Muslim history.

http://www.usc.edu/dept/MSA/quran

This Web site maintained by the University of Southern California provides three English-language translations of the Qur'an. The translations are organized by chapter; visitors to the site can also search for a particular verse.

http://www.britannica.com/EBchecked/topic/295507/Islam

The Encyclopedia Britannica's site on Islam provides information about the origins of Islam and important tenets of the faith.

http://www.crisisgroup.org/home/index.cfm?id=3301&CFID=69018069&CFTOKEN=62535824

This report by the International Crisis Group examines the different strands of Islamism in the Middle East and North Africa.

Numbers in **bold italics** refer to captions.